INLINE SKATING

www.raintreepublishers.co.uk

To order:
Phone 44 (0) 1865 888112
Send a fax to 44 (0) 1865 314091
Visit the Raintree bookshop at
www.raintreepublishers.co.uk
to browse our catalogue and order online.

Produced by
David West 🏃🏃 **Children's Books**
7 Princeton Court
55 Felsham Road
London SW15 1AZ

Picture Research: Carlotta Cooper
Designer: Gary Jeffrey
Editor: James Pickering

First published in Great Britain by
Raintree, Halley Court, Jordan Hill,
Oxford OX2 8EJ, part of Harcourt Education.
Raintree is a registered trademark of Harcourt
Education Ltd.

Printed and bound in Italy

ISBN 1 844 43089 8 (hardback)
07 06 05 04 03
10 9 8 7 6 5 4 3 2 1

ISBN 1 844 43094 4 (paperback)
08 07 06 05 04
10 9 8 7 6 5 4 3 2 1

British Library Cataloguing in Publication Data
Glidewell, Steve
Inline Skating. – (Extreme sports)
796.2'1
A full catalogue record for this book is available
from the British Library.

Acknowledgements
The publishers would like to thank the following
for permission to reproduce photographs:

Abbreviations: t-top, m-middle, b-bottom, r-right,
l-left, c-centre.

Front cover - Corbis. Pages 3, 10-11, 11, 17bl, 19,
20t, 21 both, 22b, 28b, 28-29, 29bl - Chris Hallam.
4-5, 24-25b, 27l - Adam Kola. 5t, 13b, 14bl, 23l,
25l, 26t - Buzz Pictures. 6l, 7tl & tr - Hulton
Archive. 6t - Karen Augusta, www.antique-
fashion.com. 7b - The Kobal Collection/JVC/TV
Tokyo/GAGA. 8tl, 9tr, 10, 12t, 14br, 15t, bl & br,
18, 20b, 22, 24t & m, 26b - Steve Glidewell. 8bl -
Roces Skates. 8br - USD Skates. 9br - Salomon. 9bl
- Able Hardware. 13t, 30 - Corbis Images. 27t, 29tr
- Gilles Albuge. 28l, 29ml - Pictures Courtesy of
Aggressive.com. 29br - Jess Dyrenforth/Rollerblade.

Every effort has been made to contact copyright
holders of any material reproduced in this book.
Any omissions will be rectified in subsequent
printings if notice is given to the publishers.

*An explanation of difficult words can be
found in the glossary on page 31.*

extreme sports

INLINE SKATING

Steve Glidewell

Raintree

CONTENTS

STREET SKATING
A street skater slides, or 'grinds' his skates down a handrail. Experienced skaters balance the risks of a stunt against their skills. Inexperienced skaters should not attempt this sort of stunt without full safety gear.

Introduction

Inline skating is probably the most popular extreme sport in the world. Go to any park or recreation area, and you're bound to see people inline skating. Why do they do it? For some, it's a great form of exercise - rolling on eight wheels. For more ambitious, or 'aggressive' skaters, it's the thrill of overcoming all the obstacles that cities and skateparks can offer, as they grind down handrails, walls and ledges. A lucky few can even earn a living from the sport, demonstrating their skills in thrilling competitions.

GRAB
A skater performs a 'grab', clutching his skates in mid-air.

WARNING!
INLINE SKATING CAN BE AN **EXTREMELY DANGEROUS** SPORT. DO NOT ATTEMPT ANY MOVES **BEYOND YOUR ABILITIES** AND ALWAYS WEAR THE APPROPRIATE SAFETY EQUIPMENT.

Skating on ice has been popular for centuries, but before the invention of electrically cooled ice rinks, it was a sport controlled by the weather. People wanted to be able to skate on dry land, all year round.

The need for speed

The first-known roller skates were invented in the 1760s. They had a single line of wheels, and for the next century all skates were based on this design. In 1819, a Frenchman called Monsieur Petitbled started making skates with three wheels in a line, of wood, metal or ivory. For the next 40 years, people experimented with these simple inline skates. Some skates had just two wheels and others as many as six. It was difficult to turn on these skates, and it was impossible to skate backwards on them.

EARLY QUADS
The wheels of Plimpton's skates were made of wood and were supported by rubber springs.

Roller culture

In 1863, James Plimpton revolutionized the business by putting two pairs of wheels on a skate, side by side. This was known as a quad skate. These skates were much easier to control, and the four-wheeled skate soon dominated the industry at the expense of inline skates, which practically died out. In the USA, Micajah C. Henley started to make roller skates in Richmond, Indiana, in the 1880s. He sold millions of pairs, and at its peak, his company made 15,000 wooden 'Chicago Skates' each week.

CUSHIONING THE BLOW
Before the invention of knee pads and wrist guards, people had to make do with home-made safety equipment!

ROLLER GANGS

Because there were so few cars, the street was a safer place to skate during the early 20th century – nobody attempted the sorts of stunts you see today.

FASTEST SHOW ON EARTH

Andrew Lloyd Webber's long-running musical *Starlight Express* featured singers and dancers on roller skates.

BIG SCREEN SKATING

The film business recognized the popularity of extreme sports. Inline skating has been featured in several Hollywood movies.

Evolution of the inline skate

Roller skating grew more popular during the 20th century. In the 1970s, advances in technology changed skating from a hobby into a true sport.

Dancing days

Skateboarding had been revolutionized by the invention of polyurethane plastic wheels, and roller skating soon followed. These wheels were tough, but they provided a smooth ride with the minimum amount of friction. Roller-discos opened up everywhere, with dance floors where skaters could practise their moves to the latest chart hits. In 1979, two American brothers, Scott and Brennan Olson, found an antique pair of inline skates, and decided to copy the design with polyurethane wheels. Their Rollerblade company soon became a byword for inline skating.

1819 INLINE

The very first skates had their wheels in a row, just like the inline skates of today. Monsieur Petitbled boasted in 1819 that his skates would allow people to perform the same manoeuvres on land as on ice – but these skates were difficult to turn.

WHEELS

The hardness of wheels is measured on the 'durometer' scale. The higher the durometer reading, the better the wheel is for grinding along surfaces.

GUIDE #1

This skate with large wheels is best for skating on flat ground.

WHEEL SET-UP

When skaters first thought about grinding along walls and ledges, they took the second and third wheels out of their frames, and replaced them with small skateboard wheels. Special grind wheels started to be made, which were smaller and very hard. This meant they would not obstruct the grind surface or cause skaters to stick when sliding.

Modern style soft boot

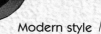

This skate has an aggressive set-up for grinds and slides.

BOOTS

In the early days of skating, there was only one type of boot – the hard boot. Now there are three main types of boot.

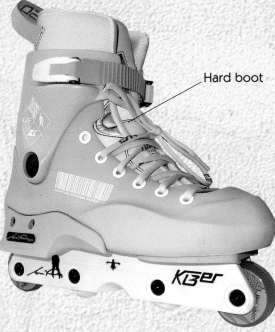

Hard boot

Grind space

Small raised plastic wheels

Frame

Hard boots Hard boots have a hard, plastic shell. They are very supportive and ideal for grinding tricks.

Soft boots These boots are very soft and flexible like trainers. They have an outside skeleton (exotech) that supports your ankles.

Hybrid boots Hybrid boots have soft and hard areas. The hard areas offer support, while the soft areas offer the flexibility you need to perform some tricks.

Hybrid boot

Frames

The frame fixes to the underside of the boot and holds the wheels. All the major skate manufacturers have agreed on the same way of fitting boots to frames, so you can swap frames and wheels to customize your skates.

When all roller skates had four thick wheels, you would never have seen the tricks that inline skaters do today. People simply cruised around, or 'free skated'. Modern aggressive skating is divided into three main styles – street, vert and skatepark.

Street skating

The idea of street skating is to 'conquer' the streets, and test yourself on its obstacles. Handrails, steps, ledges – all of these make up the skater's urban playground.

This is a challenging discipline, because skaters have to be aware of other dangers such as cars and pedestrians. If a skater, riding at full speed, crashes into a pedestrian, the results can be fatal, so it's crucial that you respect those around you. If skaters become a nuisance in a particular spot, it's likely that skating will be banned there.

🖐 STREET GRIND

A skater grinds down a handrail in an urban block of flats. Individual skaters who decide not to wear safety gear are taking a big risk.

Vert skating

Vert ramps are usually found in skateparks. They are a type of halfpipe – a U-shaped ramp. At the very top of the ramp is a sheer, vertical wall, where you can perform spectacular stunts.

Vert ramps are about 3 metres high and about 8 metres wide. It takes a lot of skill, practice and courage to tackle a vert ramp. Vert skating is probably the most eye-catching discipline in the sport, and is widely demonstrated at shows and public events.

🖐 INVERT GRAB

A skater performs an invert grab on a vert ramp (see page 18).

Skatepark

Today, there are skateparks in many towns and cities, where you'll see skateboarders and BMX riders, as well as inline skaters. The parks themselves range in size from small, outdoor facilities, run by the local council, to huge indoor parks, where you can skate all year round. Skateparks have man-made ramps and obstacles to challenge you, and the larger parks employ trained staff who can advise you on your skating, and even teach you a few new tricks.

🖐 SKATEPARK GRIND

As well as ramps, skateparks have many of the obstacles you find on the street, such as this rail.

When you first put on a pair of skates, it feels very strange – but if you learn the basics of standing up and moving off – you'll build up your confidence.

First steps

It's important to feel happy about standing still on your skates before you try to move around. You could start on a soft surface like a carpet or a lawn, and practise keeping your balance. If you walk around on your skates, as if they were shoes, you'll gradually get used to the feel of them.

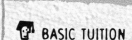

BASIC TUITION

Joining a beginners' class like this is a great way of learning the basics and meeting other skaters.

1 To get up, you should rest on your hands and knees with just the toes of your skates touching the ground.

2 As you push one knee forwards, the wheels will make contact with the ground. Raise your knee and place both hands on it.

3 Lean your weight on to your knee, and push down with your hands. As you start to rise, your other leg will naturally follow.

4 Always keep your knees bent and your weight slightly forwards to keep your balance.

GUIDE #3

HOW TO FALL

If you feel yourself losing balance, you should always try to control the fall. The shortest distance to fall is forwards on to your knee pads with your hands in front of you. If your knees are bent, this will soften the blow.

Falling forwards
Protect your face by taking some of the impact on your elbow pads.

Falling backwards
Twist around so that you're facing into the fall. Try not to trap your hands beneath you.

Moving off

Once you're confident that you can stay upright, you can start striding – gliding slowly without lifting the wheels up. If you need to steer, you can position the front skate in the direction you want to travel, while you push forwards with your rear skate. Try not to slow down by leaning backwards: there's a danger that you'll fall over backwards and hurt your lower back – one of the most common and painful skating injuries.

GETTING AROUND

Experienced skaters use their skates as a mode of transport to get them around quickly.

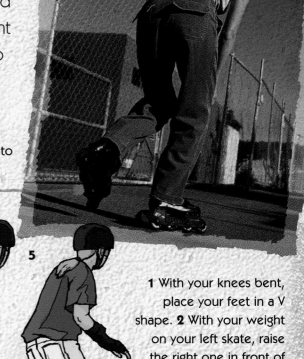

1 With your knees bent, place your feet in a V shape. 2 With your weight on your left skate, raise the right one in front of you. 3 Bring your left skate forwards. 4 Shift your weight on to your right skate. 5 Build up your rhythm, always pushing with your rear skate.

GUIDE #4

A-FRAME TURN

This is the first way that most beginners learn to turn. The trick is knowing how to shift your weight from one skate to the other.

1 Skate slowly forwards, keeping your legs wide apart.

2 If you want to turn right, lean on to your left skate.

3 Try to push the heel of your left skate outwards, and the toe inwards, without lifting the wheels.

4 Shift your weight back and stride forwards.

Stopping

At first, you'll probably skate so slowly that you'll come to a halt if you stop striding for a second. To stop – using your heel brake – you should place that skate forwards. Point your toe upwards and let the brake gently rub along the ground. Gradually put your heel down and try to keep your balance.

BEACH SKATING

Esplanades, the long, wide pavements that run alongside some beaches, have always been a popular location for inline skaters.

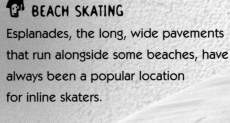

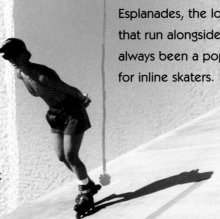

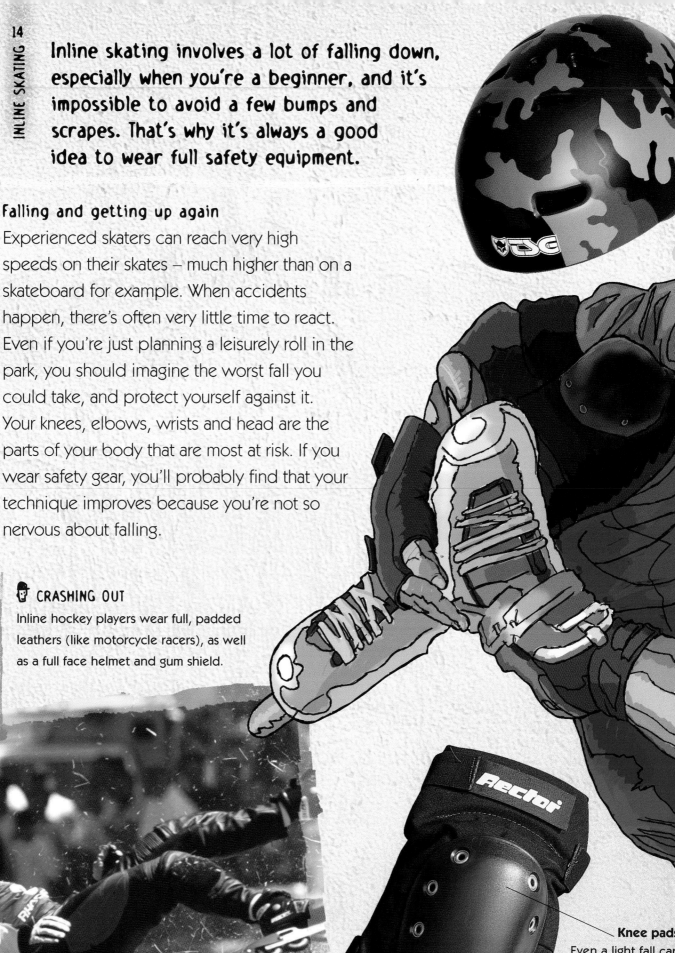

Safety equipment

Inline skating involves a lot of falling down, especially when you're a beginner, and it's impossible to avoid a few bumps and scrapes. That's why it's always a good idea to wear full safety equipment.

Falling and getting up again

Experienced skaters can reach very high speeds on their skates – much higher than on a skateboard for example. When accidents happen, there's often very little time to react. Even if you're just planning a leisurely roll in the park, you should imagine the worst fall you could take, and protect yourself against it. Your knees, elbows, wrists and head are the parts of your body that are most at risk. If you wear safety gear, you'll probably find that your technique improves because you're not so nervous about falling.

CRASHING OUT

Inline hockey players wear full, padded leathers (like motorcycle racers), as well as a full face helmet and gum shield.

Knee pads
Even a light fall can be very painful if you land on unprotected knees.

Helmet
It's important to choose a helmet that fits you perfectly. Replace your helmet if it suffers a hard knock.

VERT SKATERS
Vert skaters usually wear full safety equipment. This skater is grabbing a skate while pulling a big air.

Wrist guards
These have a solid plastic insert that absorbs the impact of a fall.

Gaskets
Vert skaters wear these under capped knee pads for extra protection.

Elbow pads
Your elbows are very prone to injury. These pads are adjusted with Velcro straps.

Basic tricks

Once you're able to skate comfortably along a flat surface, it's time to learn a few tricks. Vert, street and skatepark skaters all use the same tricks, which they adapt for different obstacles.

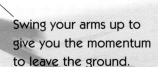

A BASIC JUMP
The most important part of any air is the landing. Before you even take off, you should check that you're not going to fall when you land.

Swing your arms up to give you the momentum to leave the ground.

Pull your knees up against your chest for a faster and higher air.

Start to straighten out again as you reach the highest point of the air.

Airs

An air is when both your skates leave the ground. When skaters go off a ramp or even jump down a set of steps, they've grabbed some air. If you perform a trick or grab while you're airborne, you can make the air look even more stylish.

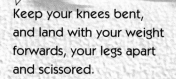

Keep your knees bent, and land with your weight forwards, your legs apart and scissored.

Spins

The name of a spin describes how many degrees you turn in the air. If you spin so that you're facing backwards, it's a 180, and turning completely around is a 360. The biggest spin ever pulled on a pair of skates is a 1260 – three and a half rotations.

HOW TO PULL A 360
Using your arms for momentum, spin your upper body around as quickly as you can. Your lower half will follow. When you reach the top of the air, check where you're going to land. Bend your knees to absorb the impact.

STALL

1 Jump on to the obstacle when you're about half a metre away from it. **2** With knees bent, lock your skates on to the obstacle and balance with your arms. **3** Push yourself firmly away.

GRIND VARIATIONS

As you become more confident, you'll be able to hold your stalls for longer periods of time.

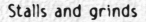

Stalls and grinds

Stalling means skating up to an obstacle, jumping on to it, staying still for a few seconds, then jumping off. The obstacle could be anything from a stair, or the kerb of the pavement, to the top edge (coping) of a sheer vert ramp. Grinding means locking any part of your skates other than the wheels on to a surface, and sliding down it. The surface could be a ledge or rail in the street, or the coping of a ramp or wall. You need to know how to stall before you can grind.

CONCRETE WALL

It is possible to grind along concrete, but it's a rough surface to land on if you fall.

Advanced tricks

You should only attempt the tricks on these pages if you are an experienced and confident skater. To avoid injury, you should wear full safety gear. With all tricks, it's important to start on small obstacles and gradually move on to bigger ones.

Flips and inverts

Flips are somersaults, backwards or forwards, where your whole body turns a complete circle. An invert is a handstand on the metal edge, or coping, of a halfpipe. To perform an invert, you need to skate into a halfpipe as if you were about to do an air. As you reach the coping and your skates leave the ramp, bend over and plant your hands on it. Your lower half will carry on travelling upwards, and you'll be facing into the halfpipe. To get down, place your feet back on the ramp and push off with your hands at the same time.

☠ INVERT

Once you've mastered the basic invert, you can hold the coping with one hand or pull a grab before you head back down.

☠ BRAINLESS

The brainless is a backflip combined with a 180 degree spin. You need to get as high as you are tall above the halfpipe, to avoid hitting your head on the coping. You'll spin quickly and cleanly if you tuck in your knees and elbows. You can slow the spin by unwinding them.

FLYING HIGH

This is a tweaked variation of the Lui Kang grab (see page 23).

(see page 23).

GUIDE #5

GRINDS GUIDE

Sweatstance
You should lock your front foot and relax your back foot, dragging it along behind.

X-grind
The X-grind is a variation of a stall. You grind down very slowly, bit by bit, with your skates at an angle of 45 degrees to each other.

Fahrvenugen
This is a difficult grind that involves bending your knees and pushing your hips in the direction you're grinding, keeping your body low.

Alley-oop Acid Miszou
Skate slowly towards the rail and spin 180 degrees as you jump on to it. You lock your front foot on to the rail and tuck your back foot behind it.

Fishbrain
Doing a fishbrain means sliding on one skate and grabbing the free skate. A freestyle fishbrain is sliding on one foot without grabbing the other skate.

Street skating

Street skating is the original form of aggressive skating. Before there were any skateparks, skaters used to roll the streets looking for obstacles like steps to jump and hills to tear down.

New challenges

Skates with four large wheels weren't up to the job of sliding and grinding. The wheels stuck to any surface you tried to grind down, and you ended up on the ground! Skates with thin, tough wheels were the answer. The 'anti-rockered' wheel system was invented – two small, hard wheels in the middle of the set-up were raised slightly so the skater could lock on to grinds and turn easily.

ALLEY·OOP

Using the large gap between the small middle wheels, this skater is performing an alley-oop (backwards) grind.

Using the terrain

With the invention of the anti-rockered system, aggressive skating was born. Street skaters looked for all the obstacles a town or city could offer, from rails and ledges to walls, or even the kerb. Today, some dedicated skaters only skate the streets, believing it to be the only true form of aggressive skating. However, skateparks also copy many street obstacles, and there's no danger to pedestrians or traffic.

HANDRAIL GRIND
18-year-old Simon Coburn demonstrates a fahrvenugen down a handrail.

LEDGE GRIND
A squared-off ledge is just as challenging as a narrow handrail.

WALL JUMP
The ability to manoeuvre anti-rockered skates means that skaters can turn easily into stunts and airs like this wall jump.

Vert skating

A vert ramp is similar to a halfpipe – both of them curve upwards on both sides. Unlike a halfpipe, the curves on a vert ramp reach a vertical angle.

Grinds and spins

The vertical face of a vert ramp measures about 1 metre, and this is where the most spectacular inline stunts are done. People ride vert ramps because they can skate more quickly and perform higher airs, pulling grinds and spins. You should know how to turn around (180) and skate backwards before you attempt vert riding, and you should definitely start skating from the flat bottom and not from the top. Inexperienced skaters can be seriously injured by dropping into a ramp. Vert skaters nearly always wear full protection.

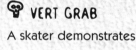

💀 VERT GRAB
A skater demonstrates a flatspin – a horizontal spin on a vert ramp.

💀 BOTTOM AND TRANSITION
Halfpipes and vert ramps are usually made of a wood called masonite. The horizontal surface is called the flat bottom. The curved arc is the transition.

Transition

Flat bottom

Vert doubles

Vert ramps are often used for demonstrations at large events and shows because they don't take up as much floor space as street courses. Crowds are thrilled by skaters flying over 4 metres in the air. In some vert skating competitions, skaters compete in pairs on the ramps at the same time. These are called vert doubles events. Skaters spin and grind over and under each other during their runs. This is a very exciting competition, but also very dangerous.

💀 **VERT AIR**
Vert ramps are usually about 3 metres high. Add a 2-metre air and you're a long way up!

GUIDE #6

GRABS GUIDE
Once you've started to catch some air, try one of these grabs to make it look more stylish.

Mute
Tuck up and grab the outside of your opposite boot.

Safety
Your arm grabs the boot on the same side, with your legs tucked up.

Lui Kang
Tuck one leg up and grab the boot, extending the other leg.

Parallel
Reach right across your body and grab the opposite skate.

That
Reach across your legs and grab the frame of the opposite boot.

Skatepark

In the 1970s, skateboarders and roller skaters homed in on empty outdoor swimming pools. The smooth, curved concrete bottom of a pool is the perfect place to roll.

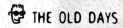

Changing fashions

Not everyone had access to an empty swimming pool, so large concrete skateparks were built. In the early 1980s these sports lost much of their popularity, and many of the concrete parks were closed. Those skaters who stuck with the sport built curved wooden halfpipes. Metal tubing, called 'coping' was used as edging on the ramps, so skaters could grind at the top. Other obstacles were grouped together to form the wooden skateparks that we know today. Many towns and cities now have indoor skateparks, so you can use them all year round. You might see BMX riders there, as well as skaters and skateboarders.

THE OLD DAYS

The ancestors of modern skateparks were simply-constructed concrete ramps in public parks.

VERT GRIND

A skater grinds along the coping (metal edge) of a quarter bowl in a skatepark.

FUN FACTORY

Skateparks have ramps of different sizes for skaters of all abilities. You should never rest on an obstacle, in case other skaters crash into you.

What to expect

As well as ramps, skateparks usually have rails and ledges similar to the type you would find on the street. Without any cars or pedestrians in sight, riding these obstacles is a lot safer though! Some skaters choose to ride only in controlled environments such as skateparks. Others use the obstacles in skateparks to invent and practise moves they can bring to the street. Skateparks often have rules about when and where you can ride. It's worth learning about these before you skate.

 MISTRAL

A skater demonstrates a mistral, edging down a rail very slowly, in an outdoor skatepark.

GUIDE #7

RAMPS GUIDE

These are examples of the most popular ramps you'll find in skateparks.

Quarterpipe

A quarterpipe is a ramp that looks like a pipe cut into a quarter.

Halfpipe

Not surprisingly, a halfpipe is twice the size of a quarterpipe. It has a sloping arc, or transition.

Fullpipe

A fullpipe is a completely circular wall. Some professional skaters can skate upside down on a fullpipe!

Hip

A hip is made up of two gently curving slopes with a sharp ridge between them. These are usually found in concrete skateparks.

Spine

The spine is a narrow ledge dividing two quarterpipes, which can be ridden along.

Competition skating

Inline skating is a naturally competitive sport. There's always a friendly rivalry between skaters who want to test themselves and impress others. Today, organized competitions are popular, too.

Three events

Just as there are three main styles of skating, there are also three main events – street, vert and real street. Each one is a test of style, creativity, difficulty and consistency.

Competitions take place in skateparks, on specially built courses, on vert ramps or even in the street.

RAIL GRIND

The obstacles in street competitions look like those in a real street.

RACING

Speed skaters wear skintight Lycra outfits so that they cut through the air as quickly as possible during races.

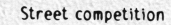

Street competition

Despite its name, a street competition takes place in a skatepark. Skaters grind along obstacles such as ramps, rails and quarterpipes. Competitors have two one-minute runs, and they try to score as many of the possible 100 points as they can. The judges are experienced aggressive skaters themselves, who know all the latest moves and how many points each competitor deserves to win.

Vert competitions

These take place on a vert ramp. Skaters have two-minute runs to use the ramp to the best of their ability. They put together a run combining grinds, airs and spins. Extra points are awarded for tricks performed well above the coping.

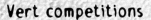 **SKATEPARK STALL**

A skater stalls on one of the safety barriers in a skatepark-based street competition.

Real street competitions

This is the latest type of competition, only introduced in 2001. Skaters can now use a real street as their competition arena. These events have been labelled I.M.Y.T.A. (I Match Your Trick Association). Specially invited skaters start on small obstacles and try to pull better tricks than the contestant before them. It works by way of elimination – the best skaters qualify to go through to the next round on a bigger obstacle.

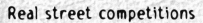 **ZIGZAG**

With gravity on their side, plenty of aggressive skaters can grind down straight rails. Not many can cope with the horizontal sections, particularly with hundreds of people watching!

Professional skaters earn a living by endorsing equipment made by particular companies, and from prize money. It takes a lot of hard work to become a pro.

Street stars

Today, most new tricks are based on street skating. So, skate companies searching for future stars to promote, are always on the lookout for creative and original street skaters. Street stars travel the world, taking part in competitions and demonstrations in skateparks and on the street.

JOSH PETTY
Josh autographs a fan's T-shirt during one of his many promotional tours.

Josh Petty

Josh Petty is from Santee, California, USA, and is known as the wild child of aggressive inline skating. His style is fast and furious and his skating always includes the latest tricks. He is sponsored by some of the top makers of skates, wheels and clothing.

Billy Prislin

Born in the USA, Billy Prislin is one of the best street skaters on the International Senate Clothing and Salomon Skate teams.

BILLY PRISLIN
Billy Prislin has recently travelled all over the world on the famous Salomon Safari Tour.

AARON FEINBERG
A star of videos and magazines, Aaron won a gold medal at the X-Games on his 16th birthday. He is now a seasoned competition skater and street skating hero.

Vert stars

Vert skaters are highly respected within the sport. It takes a lot of skill and technique even to tackle a vert ramp, let alone become a professional vert skater, competing on the world circuit. As a result, there are fewer vert skaters than street skaters, simply because vert is a more difficult discipline than street.

⚑ CESAR MORA

Cesar Mora was born in Spain but has lived in Sydney, Australia for most of his life. He has been a professional vert skater for over eight years. Cesar chose inline skating over a career as a footballer – a gamble that has paid off.

⚑ FABIOLA DA SILVA

'Fabby' was born in Sao Paulo, Brazil. She is one of the top stars of vert skating, mainly competing against men.

GUIDE #8

THE PRO LIFE

Many people want to be professional skaters, but it isn't a carefree life. Professional skaters have responsibilities to their sponsors who call on them to perform demonstrations at public events and trade shows, often at short notice. They also have to skate for photo shoots for advertising and specialist magazines, and tour for weeks at a time to promote the name of their sponsors.

On skate tours, companies often give out free samples of their products. Here, skaters are scrambling for 'freebies' given out by pro skaters.

⚑ FULL TO BURSTING

Life on the tour bus can be cramped and uncomfortable. It's not just skaters who have to fit in the bus; it's their luggage, too.

Useful information

Inline skating is popular almost everywhere, and fans of the sport are producing magazines, DVDs and video games all the time. If you have access to the Internet, you'll also find a whole world of inline skating at your fingertips.

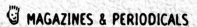 MAGAZINES & PERIODICALS

Unity

Europe's leading aggressive skating magazine. It includes features and photographs from all the best events, plus product reviews, useful advice and competitions.

The Blue Barns
Wootton
Oxfordshire, OX20 1HA, UK

Crazy Roller

Based in Paris, France, *Crazy Roller* prints stunning photographs in every issue.

16 Rue de la Fountaine au Roi
75011 Paris, France

Daily Bread

Based in San Diego, California, USA, this magazine features interviews with the best skaters and information on the latest products.

705 13th Street
San Diego, CA 92101, USA

Video Groove

This video magazine is based in southern California, USA, and is produced by Dave Paine. He takes his cameras to all the top competitions and street sessions.

UK distributor: Faze-7. Tel: 01787 269900

VIDEO GAMES

Aggressive Inline

This game was created by the software company Acclaim. It features real professional skaters, such as Sven Boekhurst and Matt Salerno. You can make them pull gravity-defying tricks.

Log on to www.acclaim.com

Rolling

Some of the best skaters in the world helped to produce this game. It features real street spots and skateparks. You can even choose what skates and clothing your character wears from the exact products you can buy in a skate shop. *Rolling* is available on all gaming consoles.

Log on to www.rollingthegame.com

USEFUL WEBSITES

www.aggressive.com
www.pure-skate.com
www.ukskateparks.com
www.roces.com
www.rollerblade.com
www.rollerblading.com.au
www.salomonstreet.com

All the Internet addresses (URLs) given in this book were valid at the time of going to press. However, due to the dynamic nature of the Internet, some addresses may have changed, or sites may have ceased to exist since publication. While the author and publishers regret any inconvenience this may cause readers, no responsibility for any such changes can be accepted by either the author or the publishers.

Glossary

aggressive
in skating, performing stunts, grinds and stalls on obstacles such as rails, walls and ramps

air
launch into the air, or leave the skating surface

anti-rocker
type of wheel set-up which has small wheels in the middle of the skate and larger wheels on the outside. This allows you to grind more easily on the area between the middle wheels.

bearings
mechanisms mounted in pairs in the hub of each wheel that make the wheel turn with the minimum amount of friction.

consistency
reliability. Consistent skaters can pull the same tricks off time and again.

coping
metal tube at the top of a ramp for grinding or stalling on

discipline
particular style of skating, such as street, skatepark or vert

durometer
measure of the hardness of skate wheels. Harder wheels have a higher durometer reading and are better for grinding. 74a is the lowest durometer reading, and 101a is the highest.

elimination
process of getting rid of entrants in a skate competition, one by one

endorsing
supporting. Professional skaters endorse certain brands of skate in return for payment.

fakie
backwards

invert
any upside-down air

manoeuvre
move

momentum
force of a moving object

prone
likely to happen

set-up
particular way a skate or its wheels are arranged for different types of skating

transition
curved arc of a ramp

x-games
massive annual competition held in San Diego, California, USA, featuring all extreme sports, such as mountain biking, skateboarding, BMX and inline skating

Index